YOUR BOAZ WILL COME

Cassandra Yvette Oliver

MyFaithToBook
.com

Author photo by Quantia Byrd

My Faith To Book
www.myfaithtobook.com

Your Boaz Will Come / Cassandra Yvette Oliver
ISBN-13: 9780692486719
ISBN-10: 0692486712

Thank you Lord for the opportunity to be a willing vessel with a willing mind for your glory!

To my sons Khalid and Kalonji: I have loved you since the first hint of knowing that you were growing inside of me. There are no words to express how much joy you have brought me and the countless moments of laughter, seeing you both grow into awesome young men. I appreciate who you have become and the growth I have witnessed internally and externally in both of you.

I thank God for choosing me to bring you forth into the world. The journey has not been an easy one but by the grace of God, we have made it. I have welcomed the challenge of motherhood and have grown in many ways to assist you in becoming all you can be. Thanks for going with the flow even when you did not fully understand what was going on in and with me. I am not the perfect mommy but I am better because of you.

Love, Mommy

CONTENTS

Acknowledgements

There are never enough words to say how much I appreciate the people who have been an intricate part of my life during the good and not so good times.

It is never an easy task to begin a work God puts into your spirit, but the work goes smoothly when people are praying for you.

Mom, thank you for planting the seed to always love God first and everything after Him.

I would like to thank Louann Overstreet, my sister in the spirit. From day one, your prayers have been fervent.

To my brother, Willie F. Simmons, for loving me just as I am and allowing me to be me.

Thanks to Apostle J. L. and Prophetess Gladys Gardner for your tireless moments of prayer and prophetic words over my life.

Mom and Dad (Apostle and Prophetess Mickie and Youwanna Saffold), words cannot express how grateful I am for the way you've watched over my soul in times of distress. Love you two always.

Pastor and CoPastor Sanders, I cannot tell you all that your ministry has done for my life since beginning this writing assignment. You have dispensed such powerful words of comfort, encouragement and grace. The development has been accelerated. Evolution is taking place daily.

To my dear friend, Pastor Richard Allen Washington Sr., for your support during the storm. You have taught me to love who I am and to build on my failures and disappointments to become the woman God designed me to be.

INTRODUCTION

A Note From The Author

The book will have moments of transparency where I reveal some real truths about challenges I have dealt with regards to relationships over the years.

I am not claiming to be an expert or a counselor, but merely a vessel being used by God to deliver this message of hope for women who have lost sight of ever being in love. I am honored to be chosen to write this most precious piece of information and revelation to you. As a writer, it gives me the opportunity to share an intricate and relevant portion of my life with Christian women—and women in general—who are seeking the face of God for a meaningful and lasting relationship with a lifelong partner.

It is my pleasure to sit and write this to you. The timing in which this book takes place is during a period when I was seeking God for my Boaz, and a time in which I was experiencing a separation from my now ex-husband, along with other various trials.

Again beloved, this book will hopefully open your eyes to some simple, yet profound principles concerning life, love, and marriage.

The story of Ruth and Boaz is such a wonderful portrait of how two people meet during seasons of uncertainty. It is a story that is a defining moment between a man and woman of God who are oblivious to the plan and desire of God.

Not only is this story about love between a man and a woman, but also about genuine love between two women who have significant ties with each other due to a season of death and despair.

The focus of the book will primarily be written about Ruth and Boaz. The union, which was ordained by God from the very beginning, will pierce your heart.

Ladies, I pray that after you read this from beginning to end, you will have a clear and vivid understanding that your Boaz will indeed come!

CHAPTER ONE

Your Boaz Will Come

I remember when I was a young girl, I had certain ideas about marriage and children. Apparently, my plans had not lined up with the plans of God. I knew that I was different from other girls, but I couldn't put my finger on it. I would attract seemingly nice young men, but found myself giving the relationship my all and getting nothing in return.

The fear of rejection would grip me to the point that I would do just about anything to get and keep a man. And I know I am not the only one who has felt this way. It is an awful truth, but real. When rejection is an issue in our lives, we fail to deal with it because we do not want anyone to know about our issue.

I remember my very first experience in college when a man noticed me, but he already had a girlfriend.

Of course, that did not matter to me at the time because I was young and had not really kept my relationship with God tight. To make a long story short, the young man and I grew close, he eventually dumped the other young lady, and we began to live together—against all that I had believed in.

He proposed and I said yes.

During the entire relationship, there was major turbulence. We were married for six months when he realized I was not what he wanted. I was devastated to the point of no return. I became a stalker. It was an awful downward spiral. I forsook God, family, and friends. I had become a woman scorned and embarrassed because I had not waited on God. We were divorced shortly after we were married, and he left me for someone else. And the cycle begins.

Drawing from the Story of Ruth

How does this apply to the story of Ruth? Well, Ruth had a personal example of a woman who lived by the scriptures and modeled what a Christian woman should be. Though Ruth and Naomi both lost their husbands, Naomi was a godly example to Ruth.

Growing up, I wasn't privileged to witness a loving and lasting marriage with in my on family. I have experienced a spirit of despair and loneliness in relationships, which God used for this moment to birth this book in my spirit.

It is no accident that my journey has brought me to this point to deliver the message of hope, for those who are patiently waiting on the Lord for their Boaz.

This is not a self-help book, but rather an inspirational story about relationship and marriage.

God has already prepared a partner for you, if you will just be patient and avoid the many separations and divorces within the Christian community.

Sometimes, as women, we do the opposite of what God says in His word: "A man who finds a wife finds a good thing and finds favor with God" (Proverbs 18:22).

Beloved, you must take heed of what the Lord says in order for your Boaz to come. It is not up to us to "find" a husband, but for the husband to find us.

I once heard an anointed man of God say, "Sometimes women repel the man God has for them." As women, sometimes we try to get our outward appearance sparkling, but we forget that our inner beauty outweighs our outer beauty. (Don't get me wrong. The outside must be pleasing to the eyes for you to compel your Boaz to come.)

It is our responsibility as women not pursue what God has not willed for our lives. We must wait on God and not force any relationship with a man. Therefore, we should never begin a relationship with someone else's spouse or partner. It will only lead to disaster for you.

Though Ruth could have had any man she desired, she was groomed by Naomi to possess the one that was truly hers. It is imperative as a woman—and especially a woman of God—to ensure that God leads your Boaz to you.

Every woman has been assigned to one man and that man only. We will find ourselves carrying the spirit of loneliness, which burdens our hearts to cause us to feel as if love will never come our way.

The critical moment during a woman's journey is when she is left standing alone to "fend" for herself. There was a time when Ruth's mother-in-law, Naomi, felt there was no hope for either one of them, but there was something she saw in Ruth: destiny, purpose, and position.

Naomi knew if she could coach Ruth to attract her Boaz, their lives could be forever changed.

Prepare Yourself

A life-changing moment in a woman's life is when she is left standing in silence.

Silence makes the loudest sound. It is in silence where God prepares you to receive your Boaz. Naomi prepared Ruth by teaching her about God.

Ladies, we must prepare ourselves during the journey of silence where resources are limited and friends and family are few.

The most intricate moments of the journey are when you are preparing yourself to receive your Boaz, who God has ordained for you.

Our eyes must be opened in order for us to envision what God has already prepared. How do we do that in the midst of everything going on in our lives? Through God's most precious words in the scriptures. This is how we begin the process of preparation.

You must study God's Word in order to understand how deeply He cares for you. Knowing this will make the journey of waiting much easier.

Stop for a moment and smile, knowing that you have value, worth, purpose, passion, and power inside of you. It is not there for you to use as a manipulative tool, but placed inside of you to arise to the occasion and prove that God is real.

God is real because He has beautifully and wonderfully made you. If there had been any doubt in Ruth's mind about this truth, she never would've gleaned in the fields.

We as women must not feel inferior when we have been asked by God to take the lowest seat. The scriptures clearly state, "In due season if you faint not you will be rewarded" (Galatians 6:9). The scriptures also state, "God will exalt you in due season" (1 Peter 5:6).

Ladies, we don't have to do the work. God has done it on our behalf, but what we must do is position ourselves through prayer, fasting, and meditation of the scriptures.

You can be the most beautiful person on the outside, but your insides are putrefied. That's like having a shiny red delicious apple, but rotten to the core. No doubt Ruth was prepared inwardly. I say that because the scriptures identify the love she had for Naomi.

When Naomi tries to force Ruth to go back with her own people, Ruth says: "Entreat me not to leave you, for I will go where you go and I will serve whom you serve."

Ruth was willing to set aside everything to follow Naomi. A word of caution to all women: Do not follow anyone who is not following Christ. Beware of the ravenous wolves that wait for you to slip up and fall so they can intercept your Boaz.

Naomi was very in tune to the Lord because of her experience serving Him. We must attach ourselves to people who know God and have experienced His goodness.

Trust in the True and Wise God

Loss does not always mean tragedy in our lives. When we are in a state of loss, it has not become our end but our glorious beginning. The loss that Ruth experienced was no doubt confusing and debilitating. Ruth was caught off guard and unprepared. Life has a way of training us and leading us into a direction we are not prepared or even ready to accept.

In November of 2013, I experienced a series of heart attacks. At 43, it caught me off guard. I was left to wonder: *Where is God leading me now?* Though concerned about my health, I was in a constant state of hope. However, I was in a third marriage, which was unhealthy and my body was not cooperating with me. I realized that every marriage I agreed to was not induced by God but my own selfish need for companionship.

Sometimes we can feel that we have finally found "the one" without really knowing who "the one" should be.

Again, scripture states that once the man finds you, he will find favor with God.

If you are single and contemplating marriage or considering a step further in a relationship, please take the time to know what God wants for you in a lifelong partner.

"Lifelong" is the keyword in the statement. Stop formulating what you think you need, but instead let God send Boaz to you. I'm so guilty of "jumping the broom" before hearing from God and waiting on Him.

Experience is the best teacher. Through my experiences, I have begun to patiently wait on the Lord because I know through His Word that He has prepared a Boaz for me and that He is preparing me even more.

Three failed marriages will teach you to wait and be selective, knowing you deserve the best from God.

I'm not saying my ex-husbands were not good men, but they were just not for me because I moved out of time with the Lord. It is my solemn duty to become as transparent in this season so that women of all ages will feel free to come to me with their burdens regarding this topic of waiting for the right man.

Ruth was confident in Naomi enough to follow her in a time of despair and uncertainty. There are times in our lives as women when we experience times of uncertainty.

The confidence Ruth had in Naomi had nothing to do with resources, material possessions, or networking. It was the inner woman of Naomi and her commitment to serving God that drew Ruth in. Ruth began to trust in the only true and wise God. It is amazing to me the choices

Ruth could have made but she chose to forsake all others—even her idol worshipping—to follow after a God who has everything.

Ruth was determined to stay with her mother-in-law to prove her loyalty and her love. In Ruth chapter 2, where Ruth first meets Boaz informally, Naomi gives her permission to ask, "Please let me go to the field, and glean heads of grain after him in whose sight I may find favor."

I imagine Ruth knew she could turn the head of any man, but there was only one she would go after.

Now ladies, please remember that Boaz was not in a relationship with anyone. We as women make the mistake of thinking, "If I can ever get his attention, he will leave her."

Don't do this, ladies! If you do, you will be headed for emotional destruction, hurt feelings, a bad reputation, and a broken heart.

Ruth went after what was clearly ordained by God. In order for her to know that, she had to have an intimate relationship with the Lord.

We sometimes skip that part to do what we want. But without an intimate relationship with the Creator, you are doomed to fail. If there is no God in your life, your life is incomplete.

No wonder there are so many failed marriages—because we do not allow God to lead us to our lifelong partner. Notice how I continually use, "lifelong partner," rather than just spouse or husband. A partner stands with you through times of turmoil and tribulation.

Love More and Live by Faith

Ruth knew within herself that she was valuable to Boaz. Boaz was an established man with wealth and notable among men within his community. No doubt a handsome man built with stature.

I can just imagine all that was going through Ruth's mind concerning Boaz. Because of the love Ruth had for Naomi, it was only fitting that she would want to share that same love with Boaz.

You cannot give what you don't have. Love is essential for any relationship. Love will allow you to bear some things that you normally would not.

Love can bring balance and cohesiveness, when things become chaotic all around you. Love is what Ruth possessed. Let's remember, beloved sisters, that love has to be given and reciprocated. We cannot expect one person to give all the love without giving any back. If you want your Boaz to come, love more.

It is important to look into the person of Ruth. What was her character? Why did Boaz favor her over other maidservants?

The first characteristic we can identify from the biblical story is that Ruth was a faithful daughter-in-law. Bound together by a bond of common grief, Ruth loved Naomi and was willing to leave her own land and share the unknown future.

It is this pivotal point in Ruth's life that prepares her for Boaz. We as women must first show ourselves to be faithful to God and His Word.

Becoming a faithful servant shows humility and aptitude. Ruth was willing to leave her comfort zone in order to gain what she clearly would not have imagined: a bright future.

Within scripture, we see that Ruth was loving and loyal. Without love being at the forefront of a relationship, it will experience insurmountable challenges.

I personally have experienced love, but did not understand that without truly loving the Lord first, I could not love someone else the way I should.

There are many forms of love that are expressed, but only one kind of love that will hold any relationship together during the storms of life.

Ruth shared that kind of love with Naomi and turned a grieving and bitter woman into a sweet example, which Ruth needed in her life.

In a society like ours—with its ever growing number of strained relationships, broken homes, and loveless lives—it is most refreshing to go back to the charming picture of loyalty found in a short yet sublime book in the Bible, which describes a beautiful example of a man and woman connecting first through the spirit, then by an appropriate physical connection.

Ruth: The Example to Model Yourself After

As we know from scripture, Ruth was a Moabite who worshipped pagan gods. In spite of her background, Ruth became a devout worshipper of the true God of Israel.

You might be wondering what all of this background has to do with my Boaz finding me. I am chuckling to myself, because I would have asked the same question.

The information on Ruth's background is an important foundation for women to take notice of and model after.

It is not merely the outward appearance that attracts the eye of a man, but the inner part of you, which overshadows the outward beauty.

What purpose would it serve to simply look good on the outside when your inner person doesn't have a relationship with God?

We are not told exactly when Ruth cast off her idolatry and turned to the blessedness of the one true God. But her newfound faith constrained her to say, "The Lord do so to me, and more also, if aught but death part thee and me."

Now, with God in her heart, she longed to live with Naomi's people, "whose God is Lord."

Ruth's decision to follow God and to identify herself with His people brought her a rich reward.

How awesome it is to receive favor for being steadfast and unmovable, always abounding in the work of the Lord!

Timing is Everything

Ruth obviously believed she was in the right place at the right time. God's timing and way is perfect. It is important to remain with the timing of the Lord. Don't step out of the rhythm of what God is doing in your life. What if Ruth had decided to turn back to what was comfortable and familiar?

I can attest that what is comfortable and familiar is not always where God wants you. Amazingly, we are under the grace of a sovereign God who gives us opportunities to position ourselves under His authority to lead us into our destiny.

It is no wonder why we often find our paths obscured and uncertain when we strike out on our own emotions, thoughts, and fleshly desires. When we begin to solely rely on God's infinite wisdom, we will certainly be victorious every time. It is a thin line between doing what God desires versus following our own ways.

I struggled with the idea of writing this particular book because I did not feel as if I would be the best candidate for the job.

One night, nearing midnight, I began to wonder if I would ever have a Boaz to love or love me. After many failed relationships and three failed marriages, I found myself weeping uncontrollably in the still of the night, when all should be at rest.

It was in that pivotal moment that God told me that my Boaz was coming. And that's precisely when God told me to write this book.

Though I felt unqualified because of my experience of failed relationships, God qualified me to share my journey with you.

As with Ruth, I can imagine she struggled emotionally, after losing her husband, brother-in-law, and father-in-law, leaving her with two women she was unfamiliar with.

I believe that oftentimes God places us in situations that are unfamiliar. But it is in those moments when God will use you, and glorify Himself through your life.

Ruth was in the right place at the right time. God's timing is everything. Even in silence, His timing is always necessary.

After many years of making my own decisions, I have learned that it is impossible to do anything without the Lord.

I understand now more than ever that if it is not time, it will not happen. It does not say in the book of Ruth how long it was before Ruth came into contact with Boaz, but we do know when Ruth was ready to be discovered, God had already prepared the way.

Women must know in advance that age and God's timing are not equal. Beloved, it is important to wait on the timing of God. The time for you to be discovered by your Boaz will be totally up to God, not you.

We must have the confidence in what God is doing in our lives in order for us to wait on Him.

I am excited about the opportunity to receive a prepared blessing made by God, just for me. No doubt, Ruth knew she was "marriage material," but it was her humility and love for Naomi that led her into that place.

God assured me many times to rest in Him. Though confident in God's Word, I felt uneasy in my spirit. I knew how important it was for me not to jump the gun again and move out of pace with God.

I am determined to truly wait on God to send Boaz to me and for me to not search for what God has prepared for me. The scriptures clearly state, "...a man that findeth a wife findeth a good thing and he finds favor with the Lord."

Always Rely on the Lord

As Ruth was in the preparation phase, she found herself working to help Naomi. It is always good for you to keep focused as you wait for your Boaz, for it is in this phase that God is preparing your heart, mind, spirit, and body.

Picture a caterpillar. One minute, it's crawling; the next minute, it's flying as a beautiful butterfly. This transition does not occur overnight, but rather it gradually changes in the midst of a dark cocoon, just as God designed it to do.

The caterpillar cannot rush the process, but rather it must wait for the appointed time of completion.

It takes patience to let God transform you into what He wants you to be.

I remember a time when a profound woman of God spoke into my life and said: "If you take care of God's business, He will take care of yours."

In other words, get busy serving the true and living God and stop worrying about your situation, because ultimately God is in control.

When I take my focus off of God, those words of advice always help me regain my focus.

I imagine that Ruth had fleshly desires. She most likely missed the touch of her husband, or wished he could be there to console her when she was sad. I can attest to those same feelings, even now as I write these words to you.

Fleshly desires can lead you away from the Lord into an area that could be difficult and challenging to recover from. Thus, it is imperative to consider the consequences that a few moments of pleasure will bring.

I know firsthand that giving into fleshly desires will cause a vicious cycle that only the Lord can rescue you from.

It is my desire to wait on God to send my Boaz, and it should be your desire as well. Aren't you tired of going in circles and coming in contact with everyone but your Boaz?

I challenge you to give the Lord an opportunity to prove to you that He is God and besides Him there is no other.

Ruth decided to follow after God and let Him lead her, through her mother-in-law. It is amazing to me how God orchestrates our lives into a symphony of high and low notes.

Ruth had experienced her time of low notes, but in a moment, we will see how her life transforms into something wonderful.

When the Holy Spirit leads you, you will receive your Boaz. It is not enough to fast, pray, and attend church services. You must have a renewed mind. This will cause you to evolve internally.

In turn, this will place you in a position to be discovered by your Boaz. Ladies, we must not be afraid to change our way of thinking and our lifestyle.

It is merely up to us to set the tone to receive God's gifts. He has already promised those who are led by the Spirit a life of abundance and peace, which works in all areas of our lives.

Take Pleasure in God

Ruth realized how important it was for her to change her lifestyle (i.e. who she served, and who she followed). It is imperative that we as woman change our patterns of living and thinking, not letting the world or others cause us to live outside of the will of God.

We must be cautious who we connect with, how we dress, and how we communicate with others. Developing the right relationships is essential to the healthiness of our spirit. As we begin to change internally, we will begin to attract God-ordained relationships.

"He that delighteth in the Lord; he shall give him the desires of our heart" (Psalm 37:4, NKJV). In Hebrew, the word "delight" means to be dependent on God and to derive one's pleasure from Him.

I am sure you are asking, "How do I delight myself in the Lord?" By doing what pleases Him and putting His words in your heart.

As we begin to honor Him with our lives through the Word, He begins to take notice of our love for Him.

Ruth was in a position to receive from God because of her change of heart from idol gods to a God who can do all things.

The idea behind Psalm 37:4 is that when we truly recognize or "delight" in the internal things of God, our desires will begin to parallel with His and we will never go unfulfilled.

1 Timothy 6:6 states: "Godliness with contentment is great gain." The world can never satisfy our deepest longings, but if we choose to delight in God's way, He will always provide above and beyond our expectations.

Ruth found that out early on in her newfound relationship with Him. We must develop an intimate bond with God and take pleasure (delight) in what pleases Him most.

Psalm 27:4 states "One thing I have desired of the Lord, that will I seek; that I may dwell in the house of Lord all the days of my life, to behold the beauty of the Lord."

Build a strong foundation and a healthy relationship with God *first*, then you will be able to share that same love with the Boaz God has for you.

The ways of the Lord are unsearchable. We can never know when or where God will reward us for our faithfulness.

Ruth was not only faithful to Naomi, but she was faithful to God, thus, He rewarded her in a way she could not imagine.

"Now unto him who is able to do exceeding abundantly above all we can ask or think according to the power that worketh in us" (Ephesians 3:20, KJV).

Our requests and thoughts are not comparable to God's. Hallelujah for that comforting word!

Connection Matters

Ruth was considered an adult, but she was subject to the wisdom of Naomi because of her connection.

Connection with the right people means success and prosperity. It is safe to say that through excellent connections, a believer can move forward in life and not be stuck in the past or stagnate in their journey.

Ruth 2:2 says, "Please let me go to the field, and glean heads of grain after him (Boaz) in whose sight I may find favor."

This verse shows the continued humility of Ruth to take a lowly job in order to provide for herself and for her mother-in-law during hard times.

It has been my experience, even now, when things become uncertain or unfamiliar, we find ourselves busy serving and not sitting idle.

As I sit and write this book, I have been out of work for three months, living with my mother with no income or possibility of work any time soon.

Since I have been off, I have helped various family members with things they may not have accomplished on their own.

In a similar way, Ruth saw a need and offered to serve in the fields, a job that most poor people did.

After Ruth heard about the wealthy relative owning the field, she believed it was her opportunity to find favor in Boaz's sight.

At times, we as women begin to settle for less than God's best. God does not deliver us scraps or leftovers. No, He offers us His very best.

Commit To Christlikeness as You Wait

Women of God cannot be with a partner that has not fully committed their lives over to Christ.

We must realize our destiny, purpose, and partner is tied up in our relationship with God.

The scripture does not expound on what Ruth was doing between the time she and Naomi arrived until the time she began gleaning in the fields.

This "time in between" is important to note. Why? Because there will be seasons in your life where you'll yearn for companionship and there won't be any.

I can imagine Ruth was experiencing that kind of season—full of waiting, aching, and loneliness. But it's what goes on between those two seasons that count.

Not long ago, God was shifting me into a familiar, but unfamiliar, area once again. It was the same scene, yet not the same.

Spiritually, I had matured and physically I had transformed. Emotionally, I was struggling but able to keep my emotions under control through prayer, fasting and meditation. The time was different. It seemed as though I had gone back into a place I did not want to be. It felt as if I was going backward, not forward.

I can picture the routine Ruth developed to formulate a relationship with a God she did not know, a God who sustained her through death, famine and uncertainty.

You might be experiencing these exact things, and you are wondering when the merry-go-round will stop spinning out of control.

You know, God will speak to your inner man and He will instruct you to rest in Him. What a feeling it is to hear God speak to you directly, and to recognize His voice and obey.

God spoke to me a few months ago, as I was toiling about work, money, children, etc. and He just simply came to me and said, "Rest in me."

I knew it was the Spirit of God because I was having sleepless nights, days of confusion, and times when I was afraid to make a decision.

Ruth may have experienced those very challenges through her period of waiting. Waiting on God is not an easy task, but through the Bible, you can find the aptitude to do so.

David said it so eloquently in Psalm 40:1, which says, "I waited patiently for the Lord; and he inclined unto me, and heard my cry."

Hallelujah! Only through the Grace of God will you begin to apply the scriptures to your particular situation.

Ruth began to read the scriptures and she heard God speak to her. It is our duty to put forth the effort to begin to search out the scriptures for the season we find ourselves in, whether self-inflicted or God-ordained.

Sometimes we can forfeit or disqualify ourselves by not adhering to the voice of God. We must run the Christian race with patience.

It does not matter when you get to the end, but *how* you finish. We are the righteousness of God and He has qualified us to receive from Him even the Boaz we are waiting for.

So do not be in a hurry to be with a partner whom is not yours.

Stand firm. Hold on to your integrity so that God may perform His good work in your life. I know you are thinking, "Easier said than done."

I have thought the same thing many times. But in order to receive all that God has in store for us, we must rely on His infinite wisdom.

Let God Take the Lead

It is a sacrifice to put all you have ever known on the back burner so that God's plans can take the forefront of your life.

Ruth knew how important it would be to put herself in a place where God could use her tragedy and turn it into triumph.

So many times when we experience difficulties in our lives, we forget God is in control of all things. Once Ruth decided to follow after God, she forsook her past and dedicated herself to her future in Christ. By doing so, God gave her what she had longed for: her Boaz.

Once Ruth received permission from Naomi to go and glean in the fields, she began a journey that will never be forgotten. It was harvest time in Israel when Boaz first laid eyes on Ruth. I can imagine the sun had painted the fields a tawny gold as workers swung sickles in even rhythms through the standing grain.

According to Israel's law and customs, the poor had the right to gather whatever the harvesters missed. Ruth toiled quickly and efficiently, stuffing grain into a sack. Strands of black hair escaped her head covering, softly framing her olive-colored skin, still smooth despite the sun. Boaz noticed her.

Gleaning was tough and dangerous work, especially for an attractive young foreigner, alone, and unprotected. But Boaz took the opportunity to give her security. Ruth 2:9 says, "You will listen, my daughter, will you not? Do not go glean in another field, nor go from here, but stay close by my young women."

Boaz shows her that he can protect her. The majority of women today desire a man who will protect them. A friend of mine once said to me, "I desire a man who will fight for me." She was not meaning in the physical sense, but in an overall sense of protection in all areas of the relationship.

I believe that statement from Boaz gave Ruth a confidence like no other. Now, ladies, this does not mean that you should go out and do something foolish to get attention.

This book is primarily written for women who are willing to change from the inside out and release what God has for them into their lives.

Boaz instructed Ruth to work in a secure part of the field with other maidservants. I believe that the women Ruth worked with were in the frame of mind that would not hinder the promise God ordained before time began.

Boaz also assured her no man in the field would touch her, and she was given permission to drink from their vessels (Ruth 2:9). Boaz displayed a wonderful example of a man's protection for his partner or potential partner. Transformation of a woman's inner person causes God to prick the heart of a man to want to secure and protect the mate God has chosen for him. There is nothing more exciting than a man and a woman feeling a connection with one another (not based on sex, money, or material things), but based on a pure admiration for each other.

I admit, every romantic relationship I've ever had was developed out of haste, fear of being alone, or the desire of my flesh. It is no easy thing to *wait*!

The waiting period can be excruciating, but it's also where God can do the most work in us. I can truly say that without Him, I would've been swallowed up in my pain. I know there are women reading this book attesting to these very words.

During the lonely anguish of waiting for our Boaz, some of us begin to busy ourselves with outside activities and increase time with friends and family, when actually God wants us to settle down so He can heal our broken spirit. Hurt can overtake anyone at any time and leave scars of guilt and shame.

I know how it feels to be broken, not by the hand of God but by my own choosing. Self-inflicted wounds are the hardest to accept because we thought that the Lord spoke in most instances. But if we had only waited for God to speak; if we had only taken the time to talk with Him; if we had just searched the scriptures for the answer, then we wouldn't be walking around beating ourselves over the head for our selfish choices.

But God says, "Be anxious for nothing, but in everything by prayer and supplication, with thanksgiving, let your requests be made known to God" (Philippians 4:6).

We must submit ourselves to a consistent and committed prayer life in order to know what God desires for us. I don't know about you, but I am waiting on my Boaz. In the past few years, I have witnessed and experienced many broken marriages because God was not at the forefront.

Don't believe the following lies:

- "He is just having hard times"
- "He will change"

Don't settle for half a man. You must truly believe that you can and will have a healthy relationship with a partner who is made just for you. Not every puzzle piece fits in the same place; therefore, not every man will fit into what God has in store for you. Every person that you chose for yourself, as I did, brought you to this particular time in your life. Every experience, though challenging, was not to harm you, but to push you to the point of lifting your hands up to a faithful God and surrendering your mind, heart, body and soul.

Do not, for any reason, drag your past into your future. But instead, take every experience and remember what to be on the lookout for. The majority of the time, we forfeit our blessing when we continue to let the past dictate how we make choices.

What to Look for in a Partner

When I received the word from the Lord to write this book, it was intended for women, but as I began to write from the scriptures, I believed in my spirit that men could benefit from this book as well. As men and women of God, we need to know what to look for in a partner.

Let us look at the story of Ruth and Boaz again. When Boaz gave Ruth her instructions (Ruth 2:9), she fell on her face and thanked him for showing her favor (Ruth 2:10). What a humble way to show how grateful Ruth was for Boaz's kindness toward her, even though she was a foreigner in the land.

The best part of this story is that Boaz had already heard about Ruth, and the good deeds she had shown her mother-in-law (Ruth 2:11). How awesome is that!

As you begin to serve and wait for God's perfect timing, your Boaz will take notice of you. Working and serving in the name of the Lord will bring multiple rewards. As David said in Psalm 103:2, "Bless the Lord, O my souls, and forget not his benefits." There are benefits for serving the Lord with your whole heart.

After Ruth humbled herself before Boaz, he pronounced a blessing over her in Ruth 2:12, which says, "The Lord repay your work and a full reward..." What a wonderful gesture! Determined to repay her kindness in some way, Boaz called to her, "My daughter, listen to me. Do not go and glean in another field and do not go away from here. Stay here with my servant girls. Watch the field where the men are harvesting and follow along after the girls. I have told the men not to touch you."

I can imagine Ruth smiling in agreement. Later, he spoke to Ruth again, this time offering bread and roasted grain for her dinner. Boaz offered security and provision for Ruth. Women of God, this is the same offering the Lord gives to us. The Bible says in Ephesians 5:25:

"Husbands, love your wives just as Christ also loved the church and gave himself for her." Boaz was showing Ruth love before they were married. Ladies, I hope you are receiving revelation as I'm writing these words. What to expect in a lifetime partner is revealed in this beautiful story of Ruth and Boaz.

Ruth was so overwhelmed with Boaz's kindness, she no doubt ran home to tell Naomi all that had happened. When Naomi heard, she began to rejoice and bless the living God for bestowing His kindness (Ruth 2:20).

As the story progresses, we find Naomi seizing the moment to ensure Ruth's security. Redemption in its truest form is in its beginning stages as Naomi informs Ruth of who Boaz is and instructs her on how to further attract him.

Beloved, you must prepare yourself to receive your Boaz. How? The preparation process includes, but is not limited to: daily reading the Word of God to renew your mind and heart, daily prayer to connect with God and hear His voice, and daily meditation to ensure you are being led by the spirit of God.

A Boaz just for You

Now, Ruth was instructed by Naomi to: "Therefore wash and anoint yourself, put on your best garment and go down to the threshing floor without being seen until he is finished eating" (Ruth 3:3).

A woman must let go of everything that has hindered her from receiving her Boaz. It is not merely enough to cast off old relationships, but to wash our hearts and minds from the relationship altogether (i.e. physical, mental, and emotional).

We have a tendency as women to want to "be the other woman" or desire another woman's partner, when those women were divinely constructed for their mates, not for us. Therefore, we must escape the confines of our own imagination and envision who God designed specifically for *us*.

If you are reading this and are currently involved with a married man, stop now! Vulnerability and hurt will cause one to be unconscious in the spirit. In other words, we abandon what God has put on the inside of us to sustain us from falling prey to the ways of the flesh.

Let me take it a little bit further. The process I am currently in is familiar in so many ways, but the difference is that I have been built up in my spirit and God has given me the strength to go through the process and not abort what he is performing in my life.

All I wanted was for the pain to go away—the pain of loss, the pain of being used for my body, and so many other hardships.

When we begin to focus on our internal pain, it takes away from what God has destined for us in the spirit. But the training received in the process is nothing more that God getting us prepared for something greater: greater responsibility, greater faith, greater revelation, and greater anointing!

I am reminded of a story in the Bible about a woman who received a son, only to lose him later in life. Yet, the woman never wavered in her faith. She believed the prophet would be able to restore her son back to her.

When the prophet's servant asked if things were well with her family, she replied, "All is well!" This simple statement, regarding her marriage and family, will prove beneficial.

Beloved, we must not forfeit what the Lord does with us during our molding process. I know that many of us try to diffuse what is going on inside of us for one moment of pleasure, but that one moment could cost a lifetime of anguish.

When God allows us to make a choice, He really wants us to choose His way. "Trust in the Lord with all your heart, and lean not on your own understanding; In all your ways acknowledge Him, and he shall direct your path" (Proverbs 3:5-6, NKJV).

When the Word of God begins to resonate in our hearts, we begin to live by it, breathe by it, and walk in it. The Word of God begins to lead us into all truth, once we believe.

I wrote this book as a means to help women reach a point in their lives where God is ordering their every move. A transformed heart and mind is the only way we will be able to truly "let go and let God." Without a renewed mindset, it will be challenging to grasp the content of these pages.

Ruth took the advice of Naomi by preparing herself to meet with Boaz again. Naomi told her what to do, specifically concerning her body. Women want a man who is physically fit and attractive, but we forget that men want the same in return.

As a woman, we must care for our bodies and ensure the temple of God is intact. It is our responsibility to be as attractive inside as well as on the outside. However, we must not be so overwhelmed with our outer appearance before we care for our inner person. The most beautiful women that I've ever met were beautiful inside and out. I know I keep harping on the inner person, but believe me, if you have not dealt with what is on the inside first, your Boaz will never come.

Looks are important, but the sweet spirit of a woman attracts the sweet spirit of a man. And we wonder why we have multiple relationships with men, which do not work. Constructing an infallible relationship with the Lord will bring incredible and amazing results in your life.

Learn from the Past

I can just imagine the excitement Ruth felt as she was preparing to meet the man God intended for her. One thing I want to say here is: We should learn from every failed relationship. Learning to take accountability for our failure gets us closer to a victorious life.

We do not like evaluating our part in a failed marriage or courtship. We tend to point the finger to take the focus off of what we may have done to "speed" up the closure of the relationship.

I have had many failed relationships, and when I look back on them, I realize that I was not totally sold out to God. If a man could take care of me physically, I was all right with just that.

Now, my focus is on spiritual connectedness, positive energy and commitment to Christ. I look deeper to decipher if what is internal will bring wholeness. Encountering a man who is godly, attractive, and charismatic is a major step towards a life partner.

Though struggles and challenges will come, the Holy Spirit in you and your Boaz will outlast the challenges facing your relationship.

It is no coincidence that God would have me write this book during my waiting process. I am flattered and honored that God would use my experiences at this moment in my journey.

I am grateful you have chosen to pick this particular book to read for spiritual restoration in the area of relationships. As I struggle even now with a great relationship with a dynamic person, it is my hope that the Lord will guide every step of the way.

Ruth depended on the wisdom of Naomi and respected her every word. It is a mighty blessing to have someone in your life who speaks to the Lord on a regular basis, a person who has revelation and understanding of who God is. This kind of connection brings clarity and empowers you with a word from the Lord.

You cannot produce fertile ground alone. It is essential to connect with a man or woman of God who can speak life into your life. It makes a world of difference between you getting your Boaz versus a counterfeit. Please take heed so that you will not waste time building connection with someone who is not your true lifelong partner.

There is nothing more frustrating for a woman than to become hopeful about a man (whom she feels is the one) only to sense God saying, "no." Women tend to base their decisions on emotions rather than hearing directly from God. Hearing from God will cause you to run into your destiny and to your Boaz.

I am convinced that every failure, every bad decision, and every misstep I've made has led me to where I am today. Everything that Ruth experienced (despair, loss, grief) positioned her for a lifetime of joy.

God Will Make Room for You

Pastor Scott Sanders preached a powerful message once where he stated, "God will make room for you!" God made room for Ruth and Naomi when their husbands died, leading them back to the place where they would meet their destiny.

When we experience hardship in our finances, relationships, or just life in general, God is leading us where He wants us to be. No matter how unpleasant the circumstances are, we must trust what God is doing in and with us. We serve an incredible God.

God's timing is unexplainable. We may never understand His ways, but we can be confident that whatever He does will be good for us. Isaiah 55:8-9 states, "For my thoughts are not your thoughts, nor are your ways my ways, says the Lord. For as the heavens are higher than the earth, so are my ways higher than your ways, and my thoughts than your thoughts" (NKJV).

Boaz entered Ruth's life at the exact right time. Their meeting was not happenstance, luck, or coincidence. It was divine timing orchestrated by God. God had already prepared the way for them to meet, before they were even conceived in their mother's womb.

Jeremiah 1:5 states, "Before I formed you in the belly, I knew thee." God knew the day Ruth would lose her husband and gain the husband who would change her life.

Ruth and Boaz were bound to meet because God ordained it. If you are a single woman in waiting, keep waiting until God sends your Boaz to you. The benefit of waiting is twofold: 1) God begins to prepare you and 2) God prepares your partner for you.

If we look deeply into the story of Ruth and Boaz, we will see more than a love story, but of sowing and harvesting. In order to get what God has for you in a partner, you must be willing to totally give yourself to the Lord. There is no victory without sacrifice.

Naomi was careful to give Ruth the best instructions to bring security into her life. No doubt Naomi knew Boaz to be a well-known man, who was of the same household as she. Naomi told Ruth, "Therefore wash yourself and anoint yourself, put on your best garment and go down to the threshing floor; but do not make yourself known to the man until he has finished eating and drinking" (Ruth 3:3).

Such wise counsel from a woman of God. The most important turning point in Ruth's life was about to happen. We as women feel men should accept us the way we are, which is true to a certain extent.

If you look at the book of Esther, you will find she did the same act before making her request known to the King. She bathed in anointing oils before approaching her husband. This is so indicative of how Christ was placed in a tomb and anointed with sweet spices by the women, then, as we know, He was resurrected on the third day.

Beloved, remain in sync with your inner woman and take appropriate measures to maintain your youthfulness inside and out. Anointing yourself puts you in a place where God can approve and receive who you are.

Ruth had prepared to present herself to Boaz in a more formal and intimate way. (Women normally stayed clear of the threshing floor during the evening festivities when men celebrated the harvest with food and drink).

Once the feast had died down, Ruth approached the spot where Boaz was sleeping, uncovered his feet, and laid down. At midnight, Boaz became startled at the sight of a woman at his feet. How many of us have been awakened by God in the midnight hour for Him to give us a word regarding the next level of our journey or process or to bring clarity and revelation to a challenge we are experiencing?

I know there are women who have cried themselves to sleep in the midnight hour with a broken and contrite spirit. But we know that our God never sleeps nor does He slumber.

Crying is not an act of weakness, but of strength, when we are seeking mercy and direction from the Most High God. Boaz asked Ruth, "Who are you?" And Ruth replied, "I am your servant." But the tenderness of his response to Ruth was: "The Lord bless you, my daughter! For you have shown more kindness at the end than at the beginning, in that you did not go after young men, whether poor or rich."

Boaz was impressed that Ruth had refrained from any other romantic relationship, both physically and emotionally.

1 Peter 1:5 states, "Who are kept by the power of God through faith for salvation ready to be revealed in the last time." This scripture is letting us know that only through the power of God can we resist the temptation of the flesh.

Once I was tempted like never before and wanted to give in, but the power of the Holy Spirit helped me to overcome the urge to give over to my flesh.

Beloved, we sometimes forget the power God gives us to overcome the temptations and fleshly desires which are presented to us daily.

Because Ruth was a woman with a spirit of humility, she did not take the opportunity to rush to Boaz, but instead daily performed her responsibilities in the field.

Boaz offers a wonderful portrait of a great man. He showed extraordinary generosity and kindness to a young widow who came from a foreign land. He went out of his way to make sure Ruth would be safe and that she would gather a bountiful harvest.

Rather than being offended by her unconventional offer of marriage, Boaz considered it more evidence of her kindness. He is the type of man God promises to bless us with.

Boaz was a man going about his everyday work when God brought an unexpected blessing into his life. Boaz was someone of great standing in Bethlehem, a man who may have been content with life the way it was.

He was also a man of intelligence and with a high code of morals; he appreciated Ruth's quiet loveliness, her inborn purity and generosity of soul. Boaz began to shower Ruth with small favors upon her.

As women, we become emotionally attached to a man before God has spoken in our spirits the very thing we need to do. I find in many relationships, women begin to shower the man with gifts before he can get an opportunity to show his appreciation. Because women have not nurtured themselves properly, they begin to nurture the man in order to "keep" him. It is not the physical that will attract a man of God, but a quiet and humble spirit. The Bible says, "For the LORD takes delight in his people; he crowns the humble with victory" (Psalm 149:4, NIV).

Ruth 3:10 shows Boaz's gratitude towards Ruth's patience to not go after a younger man whether rich or poor. This statement somewhat indicates that Boaz was an older, more seasoned gentleman who felt Ruth really wanted to be a part of his life because she did not go after perhaps a younger, more vibrant man.

Boaz blessed her and asked her not to be afraid in verse 11, where he says, "Do not fear, I will do for you all that you request, for all the people of my town know that you are a virtuous woman."

Boaz was ready and prepared to do what Ruth asked of him. Beloved, we must find ourselves in a spirit of humility and let the man be the man, as long as he is following Christ and walking under the auspices of the Holy Spirit.

It is important to understand that it is acceptable for a woman to be independent, but there is nothing sweeter than a woman who can relax and be vulnerable to the kindness of a man and accept his offering with a humble heart.

When God sends Boaz to you, you must be willing to submit to what you asked God for. One attribute that Boaz possesses is kindness. When a true man of God approaches you, he will be kind to you and respect the God that is in you.

Boaz was very clear on what kind of woman Ruth was by watching her daily in the fields. Boaz also called her a virtuous woman—a woman of moral excellence, goodness and righteous, conforming to ethical and moral principles.

Can you find yourself in that description of a virtuous woman? If you can, you are well on your way to being prepared to receive your Boaz.

According to Strong's Exhaustive Concordance, the word translated here as "virtuous" is a Hebrew word that can best be translated in English as "chayil," which means army, wealth, valor, strength, great forces, might and power.

As you read the book of Ruth, you find that the description of a virtuous woman fits Ruth very well. Did that happen overnight? No! Some of the attributes she was born with, and others were developed over a period of time as she began to formulate a relationship with God.

I pray that as you're reading, you are receiving the revelation of why this book was written. As for me, I do believe I have some of Ruth's attributes, but only over the course of every challenge, experience, and disappointment did they really become a part of who I am today.

Your Boaz will Lead You

Fourteen years ago, it was not about being a virtuous woman, but just a woman in general. I thought I possessed good qualities and I loved God, but that was not enough to receive the man God had prepared just for me.

We strive to attract a man that is the whole package, but fail to realize the man is looking for the same thing. Ruth was preparing every day, up until she was instructed to make her way to the threshing floor where her destiny would be fulfilled.

Upon a little research, I read that the threshing floor was a place of blessing, a place where what had been planted has been harvested and the grain separated for food.

In verses 12-18, we find Boaz taking his leadership qualities and putting them to work by giving Ruth sound advice. First, Boaz instructed his servant not to let it be known that Ruth had come to the threshing floor during the night hour because there might be idle gossip. He was also aware that there was a closer relative than himself, one who would have a prior claim to Ruth. Boaz instructed Ruth to "stay here for the night and I will go to see if he wishes to redeem you for himself."

There are powerful moments in those few scriptures where Boaz shows his confidence in who God made him to be: the head. The Bible clearly states in Proverbs 18:22: "He who finds a wife finds what is good and receives favor from the Lord."

A man must be confident in God and himself in order to lead a woman in the direction of wholeness. One cannot find fulfillment in what a man possesses materially, but what he possesses spiritually.

Boaz went up to Bethlehem shortly after speaking with Ruth and sat at the town gate until he found the man he was looking for.

Ruth 4:1-4 states: "Now Boaz went up to the gate and sat down there, and behold, the close relative of whom Boaz spoke was passing by, so he said, 'Turn aside, friend, sit down here.' And he turned aside and sat down. He took ten men of the elders of the city and said, 'Sit down here.' So they sat down. Then he said to the closest relative, 'Naomi, who has come back from the land of Moab, has to sell the piece of land which belonged to our brother Elimelech. So I thought to inform you, saying, 'Buy it before those who are sitting here, and before the elders of my people. If you will redeem it, redeem it; but if not, tell me that I may know; for there is no one but you to redeem it, and I am after you.' And he said, 'I will redeem it.'"

Boaz was a clever businessman. When you are in a marriage or a serious relationship, the man has been divinely created on purpose to lead the family. The one thing that disturbs my spirit is when a man sits back and waits for the woman to make all the decisions.

Women, the majority of the time, desire a partner who will lead the family into purpose, prosperity, and power. Boaz was a leader by nature, created by God to lead and have dominion.

I have been in relationships where the man did not possess half the qualities that Boaz did, but I went with it, hoping what I was seeking would come. But my relationship with God was not strong, therefore I settled because of where I was spiritually.

A mature man of God is what we should all seek out and wait for. One of my favorite scriptures is Hebrews 10:23, which says, "Let us hold fast the confession of our hope without wavering, for he who promised is faithful."

Beloved, if you are hoping for your Boaz and believing with everything in you, God will be faithful to deliver. Boaz gave the relative the rest of what went with the land. Ruth 4:5 says, "On the day you buy the land from Naomi and from Ruth the Moabites, you acquire the dead man's widow, in order to maintain the name of the dead with his property."

As though pulling his hand from a hot stove, the relative immediately withdrew his offer, saying, "I cannot redeem it because I might endanger my own estate. You redeem it yourself."

Boaz publicly declared his intention of buying the land and marrying Ruth. And the elders, who were witnesses to the transaction at the gate, pronounced a blessing over what took place by saying, "We are witnesses. May the Lord make the woman who is coming into your home like Rachel and Leah, who together built up the house of Israel. May you have standing in Ephrathah and be famous in Bethlehem. Through the offspring the Lord gives you by this young woman, may your family be like that of Penez, whom Tamar bore to Judah."

Boaz received favor from God when he conducted his business properly, gained a wife, and received a pronounced blessing over his life and his new wife, Ruth, and their children. What an awesome ending and beginning after all Ruth had endured and experienced. Through it all, she never wavered. She remained poised and confident, and she received favor from the Lord.

Stay Strong

Ladies, we must begin to speak life into every situation we experience. It is a very good thing to pray, but a greater thing when you begin to speak what you see or hope for from the spirit realm. If you desire a Boaz to come into your life, you must speak or declare or command him to come into your life.

But do not just do it for a week or a month. Speak it until He manifests it into your presence. Don't speak it if you are not going to believe that God will provide a man for you.

Time is not a factor while you are speaking. But while you are speaking, build a strong and satisfying relationship with your God. If you are requiring a Boaz, just know Boaz is requiring a Ruth.

So Ruth and Boaz were married. Boaz, a man wise enough to know a good woman when he saw one, recognized the blessing God had granted to him for his faithfulness. Ruth soon bore him a son named Obed. Obed became the father of Jesse, and Jesse became the father of many sons, including the great King David.

Boaz was the living embodiment of the person who heeded the counsel of Philippians 4:8-9, which says, "Finally, brothers, whatever is true, whatever is honorable, whatever is just, whatever is pure, whatever is lovely, whatever is commendable, if there is any excellence, if there is anything worthy of praise, think about these things. What you have learned and received and heard and seen in me practice these things, and the God of peace will be with you."

Sometimes we connect with a man through a friendly meeting and discover that they are all that we desire in a mate. The friendship is strictly platonic—no interest in physical contact—but just a strong connection, which leads to a desire when you are only meant to be friends.

I have experienced this during my journey. A connection with the opposite sex does not always mean a permanent fixture in your life. I have realized that when we hold on to a temporary fixture, we block what God is trying to get to us. I can sing with the choir on this one.

I have a friend whom I love dearly, and he is everything I desire in a man, but he is spoken for. And I realize that along my journey, I will meet men who fit the bill but are indeed not for me. If this happens to you, know that you should not covet, but admire.

Moments of loneliness may cause you to move out of the will of God, but I am a firm believer that when it is time, it will be yours. Remember to dive into the Word of God and seek out that which God desires for you. Tell Him the qualities you are seeking in your Boaz, but make sure you are first where you need to be (spiritually, emotionally, and physically) before laying your desires before Him.

You cannot receive that which you are not prepared for. What a challenge to singles, widows or divorced women to take on while juggling everything else. Balance is key to receiving what God has for you. A virtuous woman must know how to balance everyday life and challenges without seeming on edge. God is the ultimate balance for all who seek after Him.

Beloved, do not let "eye candy" cause you to lose out on your Boaz. Stay focused on God and He will be faithful. God is able to restore and redeem the time you feel you have lost waiting.

Ladies, age is not a determinant for God. He will do it in His own time. Patience is required when we depend totally in God. You cannot be weak when seeking after God and His promises.

Find strength in God.

Endure and prepare to receive His blessings over your life, including your Boaz.

About The Author

Cassandra Yvette Oliver is known for her trust in the Lord. Through many experiences and challenges in life, she has learned to trust God in all things. She has lived in Southwest Georgia for most of her life, reared in the church and serving in many capacities over the years. She learned about God at a young age and gives credit to many men and women of God who trained and nurtured her throughout her Christian journey. She began teaching adult Sunday school classes in her uncle's ministry at the age of 17, and continues to use her teaching gift when the call arises. Cassandra is currently serving at Rhema International Ministries, Albany, Georgia under the leadership of Pastor and Co-Pastor Cynthia Sanders. Cassandra has served for over 28 years in the church using her ministry gifts to help advance the kingdom of God.

Cassandra graduated from Lowell High School in 1988. She currently holds a Bachelor of Arts degree in Organizational Leadership received in 2010 and a Master's of Science degree in Nonprofit Management received in 2012. She is the member of a great sorority, Zeta Phi Beta Sorority, Inc. and the National Professional Women's Association. Cassandra has successfully achieved her educational desires and is striving to advance in her personal and spiritual goals.

Cassandra is a single mother of two sons, Khalid and Kalonji. Her motto for life is, "Live, Laugh, and Love." One of her favorite scriptures is 1 Peter 5:10: "And the God of all grace, who called you to his eternal glory in Christ, after you have suffered a little while, will himself restore you and make you strong, firm and steadfast" (NIV).

www.ingramcontent.com/pod-product-compliance
Lightning Source LLC
Chambersburg PA
CBHW072054040426
42447CB00012BB/3120